ABC Wipe-Clean Activity Book

for ages 3-5

This CGP wipe-clean book is full of colourful ABC activities for Pre-School and Reception children.

It's a fun way to introduce the essential skills — and you can wipe it clean to enjoy again and again!

Hints for Helpers

Here are a few useful things to know when using this book:

- Your child can use the pen provided to write or draw their answers. They can use their right or left hand — whichever they find easier. The pen can be wiped away with a cloth once they've finished a page to allow multiple chances to practise.

- Keep the pen away from your child's eyes. Avoid getting the ink on clothing, furniture or fabric as it may not be washable.

- This book contains practice to help children learn to recognise the letters of the alphabet. You can help your child by reading the instructions out loud and encouraging them to sound out letters.

- It is often helpful to use letter sounds with your child, rather than letter names, as children learn letter sounds in specific ways at school. For example, if you see the letter 'n', you should say 'nn', not 'en'. It's a good idea to consult their school's phonics program or teacher for advice.

- For each letter, there is a dot showing where to start and arrows to follow to complete the letter.

- Bear in mind that every nursery or school has its own handwriting style. Some schools may form letters differently to how they're written here — for example, k instead of k.

- This book is designed to be worked through in order. However, the 'Zoo roundup' activity in the centre uses letters from the whole book. You may want to complete this activity last.

Contents

The letter a	2
The letter b	3
The letter c	4
The letter d	5
The letter e	6
The letter f	7
The letter g	8
The letter h	9
Zoo roundup	10
The letters i and j	12
The letter k	13
The letter l	14
The letters m and n	15
The letter o	16
The letters p and q	17
The letter r	18
The letter s	19
The letters t and u	20
The letters v and w	21
The letters x, y and z	22

Published by CGP

Editors: Hannah Lawson, Duncan Lindsay, Gabrielle Richardson

With thanks to Keith Blackhall and Gareth Mitchell for the proofreading.

With thanks to Alice Dent for the copyright research.

ISBN: 978 1 78908 968 4

Printed by Elanders Ltd, Newcastle upon Tyne.

Graphics used on the cover and throughout the book © Educlips
Cover design concept by emc design ltd.

Text, design, layout and original illustrations © Coordination Group Publications Ltd. (CGP) 2023
All rights reserved.

CGP, Broughton House, Griffin Street, Broughton-in-Furness, Cumbria, LA20 6HH

CGP c/o Elanders GmbH, Anton-Schmidt-Str. 15, 71332 Waiblingen, GERMANY
info@elanders-germany.com

Photocopying this book is not permitted, even if you have a CLA licence.
Extra copies are available from CGP with next day delivery • 0800 1712 712 • www.cgpbooks.co.uk

The letter a

First Try This

The letter **a** starts with a round shape.
Practise writing the letter **a** below.

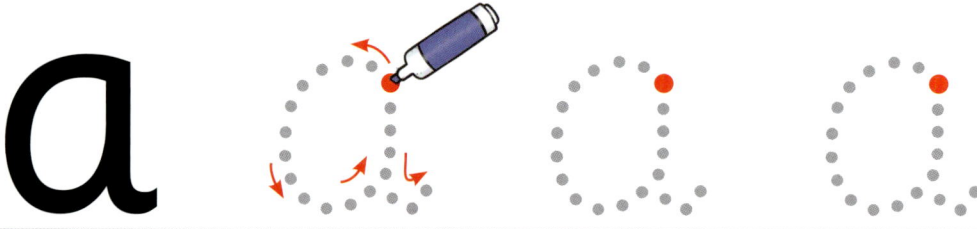

Now Try This

Practise writing the letter **a** in the words below.
Draw lines to match the words to things in the classroom.

You can write the letter a! Draw a smiley face.

The letter b

First Try This

The letter **b** has a straight line and then a loop. Practise writing the letter **b** below.

b b b b

Now Try This

Practise writing the letter **b** in the words below. Then, trace the patterns on the snails' shells.

bee

web

bug

Brilliant work — you should be proud. Draw a smiley face.

The letter c

First Try This

The letter **c** is a curve.
Practise writing the letter **c** below.

c c c c c

Now Try This

Practise writing the letter **c** in the words below.
Draw lines to match the words to the pictures.

cat

cage

duck

You're super at writing the letter c. Draw a smiley face.

The letter d

First Try This

The letter **d** starts with a loop.
Practise writing the letter **d** below.

d d d d

Now Try This

Practise writing the letter **d** in the words below.
Trace the missing objects to complete the picture.

dry dig

mud

You're doing really well! Draw a smiley face.

The letter e

First Try This

The letter **e** is curly.
Practise writing the letter **e** below.

  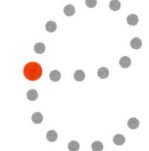 

Now Try This

Practise writing the letter **e** in the words below.
Draw a line to match the two words that rhyme.

   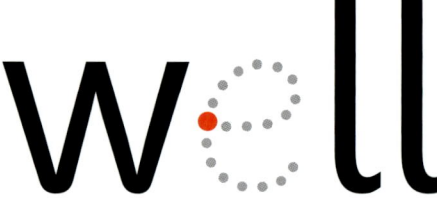

ar   **k y**

Excellent work with the letter e. Draw a smiley face.

The letter f

First Try This

The letter **f** starts with a curved line.
Practise writing the letter **f** below.

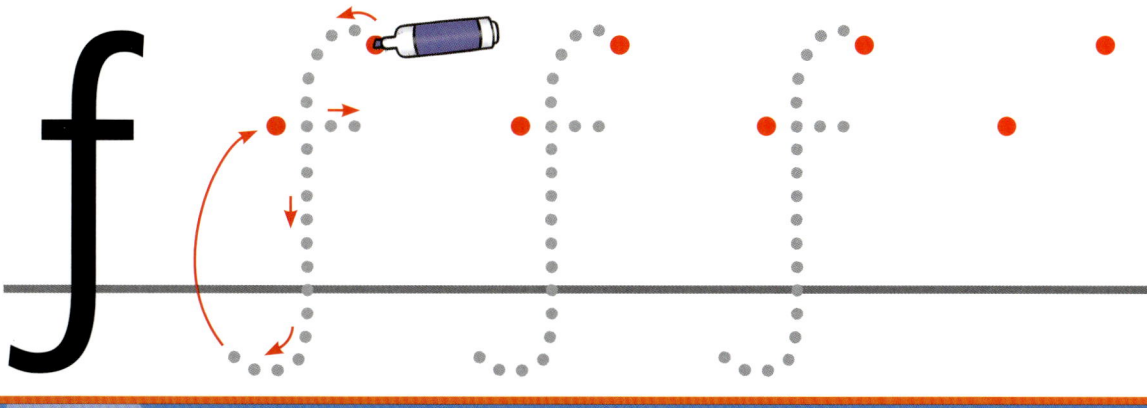

Now Try This

Practise writing the letter **f** in the words below.
Then, put out the fire by drawing water from the firefighter's hose.

You're fantastic at writing the letter f. Draw a smiley face.

The letter g

First Try This

The letter **g** starts with a loop.
Practise writing the letter **g** below.

Now Try This

Practise writing the letter **g** in the words below.
Draw lines to match the words to the right pictures.

do**g**   **g**oat   pi**g**

Keep up the good work! Draw a smiley face.

The letter h

First Try This

The letter **h** has a straight line and a curve. Practise writing the letter **h** below.

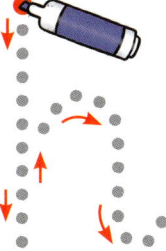
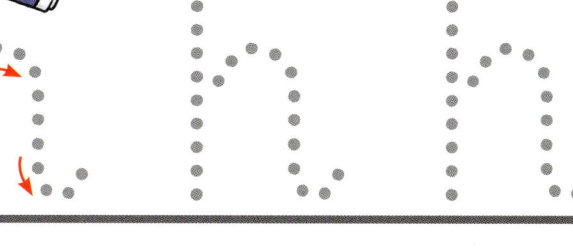

Now Try This

Practise writing the letter **h** in the words below.

hat   her   his

Circle the cakes with the letter **h** on them.

If you're happy with the letter h, draw a smiley face!

Zoo roundup

Oh no — the animals have escaped from the zoo! Trace the words, then draw lines to match them to the correct animals. There will be one animal with no word attached to it. Draw a picture of it in the box on the right.

You will need letters from the whole book to do this activity.

zebra

lion

The letters i and j

First Try This

The letters **i** and **j** have a dot on the top.
Practise writing the letters **i** and **j** below.

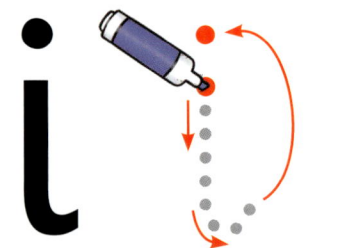

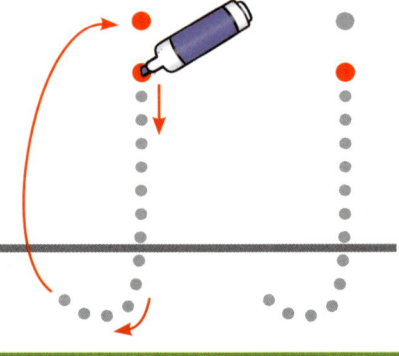

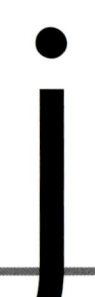

Now Try This

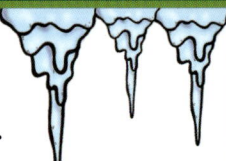

Practise writing the letters **i** and **j** in the words below.
Then, trace the umbrella handles to complete the picture.

mist   joy   ice

jump

wind

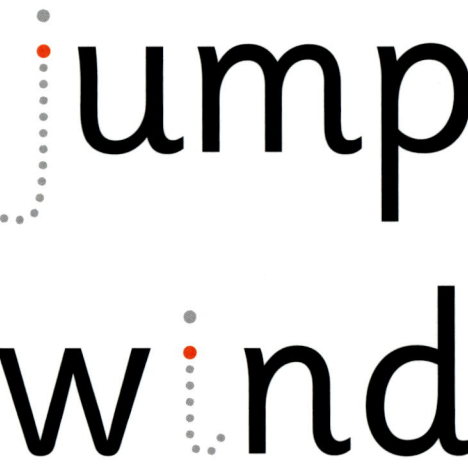

Amazing work! You know the letters i and j. Draw a smiley face.

The letter k

First Try This

The letter **k** starts with a straight line.
Practise writing the letter **k** below.

k k k k

Now Try This

Practise writing the letter **k** in the words below.
Then, circle each letter **k** on the board.

kid

sky

ink

ask

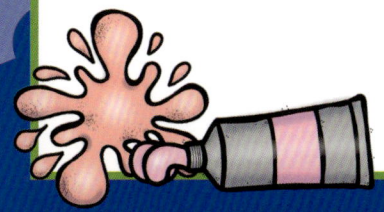

Another letter learnt — awesome! Draw a smiley face.

The letter l

First Try This

The letter l is a straight line with a flick.
Practise writing the letter l below.

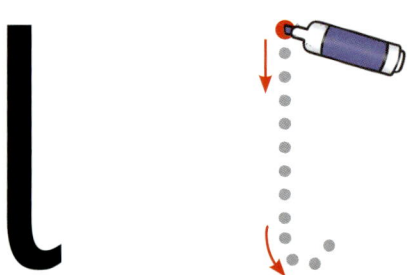

Now Try This

Practise writing the letter l in the words below.
Then, draw lines to match the words to things in the park.

slide

flag

lion

You've learnt the letter l. You're a legend! Draw a smiley face.

The letters m and n

First Try This

The letters **m** and **n** start with a straight line. They go down, then back up and over. Practise writing the letters **m** and **n**.

Now Try This

Practise writing the letters **m** and **n** in the words below.

Trace the lines to complete the picture. What can you see?

Nice work with the letters m and n! Draw a smiley face.

The letter o

First Try This

The letter **o** is a round shape.
Practise writing the letter **o** below.

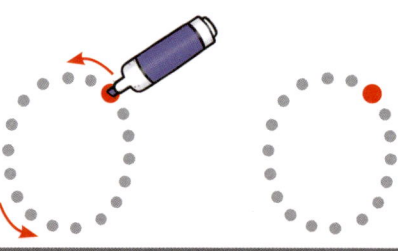
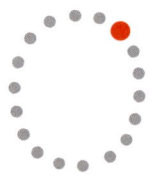

Now Try This

Practise writing the letter **o** in the words below.

old   boat   out

Circle two objects on the beach that look like the letter o.

You know the letter o — bravo! Draw a smiley face.

The letters p and q

First Try This

The letters **p** and **q** both have a straight line and a loop. Practise writing the letters **p** and **q** below.

Now Try This

Practise writing the letters **p** and **q** in the words below. Circle the picture that matches the word it's attached to.

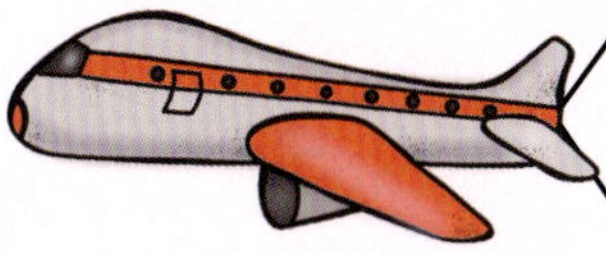

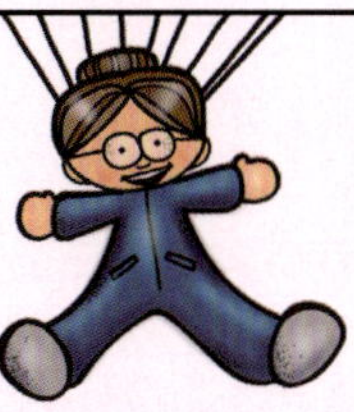

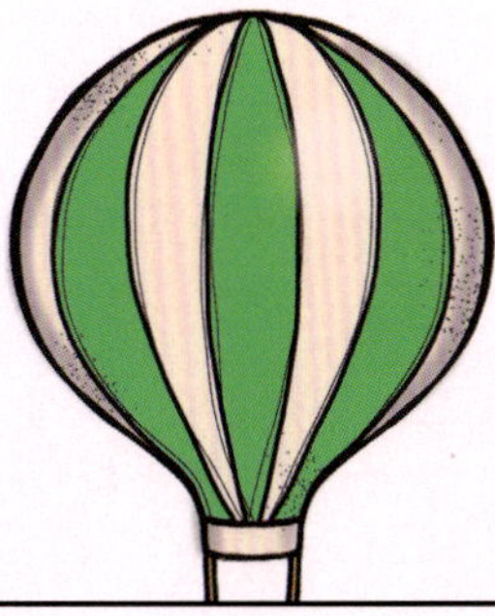

You flew through this page! Draw a smiley face.

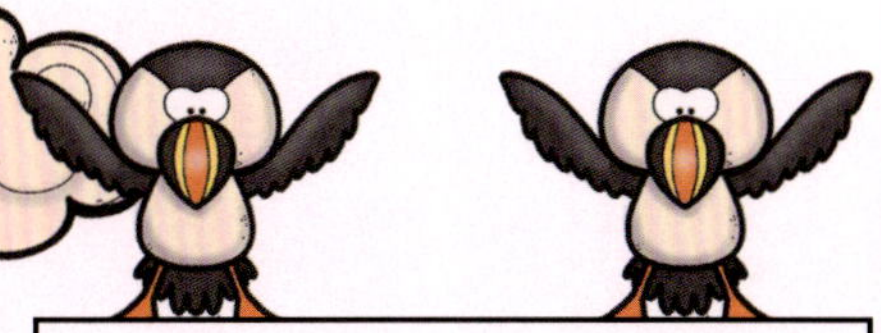

17

The letter r

First Try This

The letter **r** starts with a straight line.
Practise writing the letter **r** below.

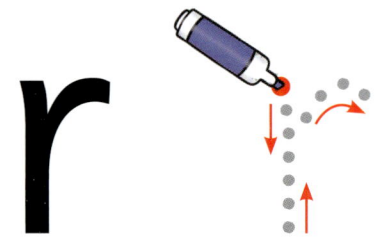

Now Try This

Practise writing the letter **r** in the words below.
Circle two words that describe the gift Simon is giving to Ava.

rose   star

car   red

You're a pro at writing the letter r. Draw a smiley face.

The letter s

First Try This

The letter **s** is curly.
Practise writing the letter **s** below.

S s s s

Now Try This

Practise writing the letter **s** in the words below.
Then, draw lines to match the words to the correct pictures.

snake   nest

stones

You're speeding to success with the letter s. Draw a smiley face!

The letters t and u

First Try This

The letters **t** and **u** both have straight lines and curves. Practise writing the letters **t** and **u** below.

Now Try This

Practise writing the letters **t** and **u** in the words below.

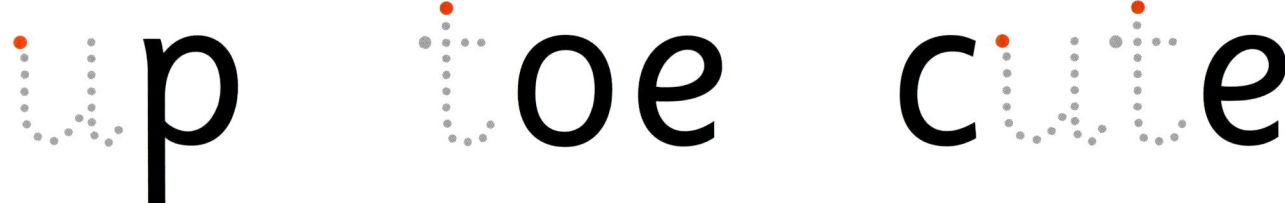

Draw smiles on the monsters to complete the picture.

You did a frightfully good job! Draw a smiley face.

The letters v and w

First Try This

The letters **v** and **w** are both pointy.
Practise writing the letters **v** and **w** below.

Now Try This

Practise writing the letters **v** and **w** in the words below.
Trace the zig-zags to connect the words to their pictures.

You're a whizz at the letters v and w. Draw a smiley face.

The letters x, y and z

First Try This

The letters **x** and **z** are pointy. The letter **y** has straight lines and curves. Practise writing the letters **x**, **y** and **z** below.

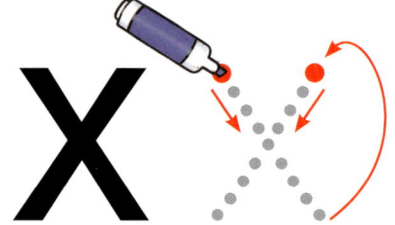 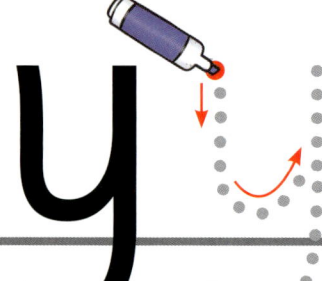 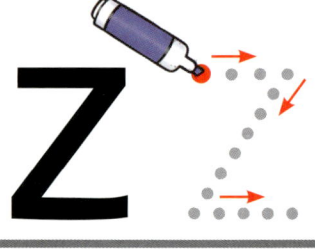

Now Try This

Practise writing the letters **x**, **y** and **z** in the words below. Then use the grid to play noughts and crosses with a partner.

 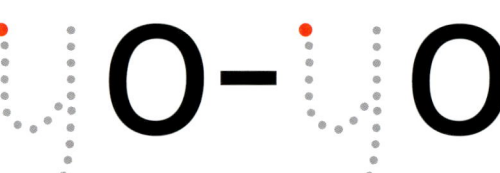

 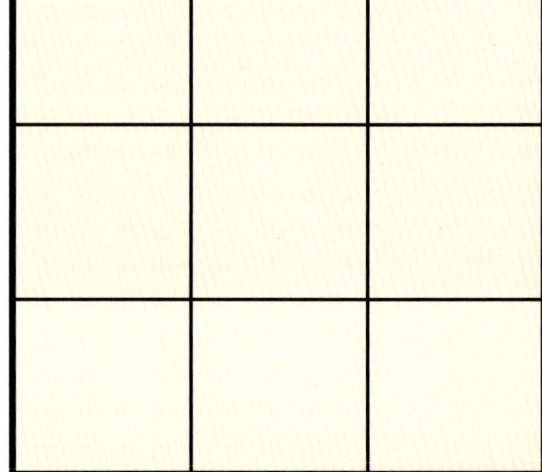

Great work — you're an alphabet hero! Draw a smiley face.